A BEGINNER'S GUIDE TO BUSINESS
WITHOUT THE FLUFF

SHUT UP AND
STARTUP

DAMIÓN HOLLOMON

DOWNLOAD THE
SmartPhoneRecords
App

www.SmartPhoneRecords.com

Sell your music (or any audio file)

straight from your smartphone worldwide.

Copyright © 2015 Damion Hollomon

Published by November 15th Publishing House

www.ShutUpandStartupBook.com

First edition

Cover Designed by Rob Williams fiverr.com/cal5086

Edited by Reyna Carrasco

For information regarding special discounts for bulk purchases, please contact
bulksales@shutupandstartupbook.com

ISBN-13: 978-1519625953

ISBN-10: 1519625952

This book is dedicated to

All the startups in the struggle, my parents and my better half, Reyna.

| Contents |

Part III - The Launch

INTRODUCTION

I want to begin by saying that this book won't be your typical "how-to" business book. I didn't graduate from a prestigious business school but I have gained a great deal of business savviness from what some refer to as the "School of Hard Knocks," also known as "life." I did receive a Bachelor of Science degree in International Business from Morris Brown College, but to be completely candid, I've learned more from actually participating in business than I ever did in any structured classroom setting. Having gained a substantial amount of experience through my own business ventures by traveling the world and working closely with people from all backgrounds and cultures, it were these moments that helped prepare me to eventually launch my own startup, SmartPhoneRecords.

My intention for this book is not that it be viewed as a mere lecture about rights and wrongs, dos and don'ts. Rather, I'd prefer that it be absorbed as a dialogue between two friends, as though you are asking the questions and I share what I've learned up to this point. I am, by far, not an expert and I don't claim to have all the answers, but I do believe my input can be helpful to those who have the desire to start their own business but have no prior business experience nor a clue where to begin.

Lastly, the opinions and guidance provided in the following pages are strictly based on my own personal experiences. Neither are intended to represent every business situation and should not be acted on as such without first seeking qualified professional counsel in relation to your individual circumstance.

~Why Did I Write This Book?~

For one, I wanted to write something for my peers. There are countless books on the market that tell people how to run startups or create a business and many are filled with useful information. But as a first-time, aspiring entrepreneur I frequently ran into a couple of problems. One, they were saturated with information that I wasn't quite ready for and two, I had to sift through mounds of "fluff" just to find the information I needed. Since I am writing this book as if I were talking to a friend, for this very reason, I won't give you useless information or have you jump through unnecessary hoops in order to get you started. Instead, I want to pass along to you the more practical steps I took that can still lead you in the direction you wish to go.

Secondly, I wanted to bring a new culture to the startup world. There are millions of ideas floating around out there that the world will never get to experience because their owners think their current climate is not ideal; in other words, not having the proper resources, not living in the perfect location or knowing the right people. These are just a few of the reasons that stop many people from starting a business and such misconceptions are precisely why I felt the need to write this book.

Another reason was because I simply wanted to experience the process of book writing. It has always been on my "bucket list" and I believe something magical happens when you actually experience a process from concept to creation and then creation to customer. You partake in something that no one can ever take from you and that is expressing your thoughts through literary means. That's one great beauty of writing a book--it will outlive you, and your words can always be relevant no matter how much time passes.

Lastly, I felt compelled to write a book because I believe I have a business perspective that is unique and can help people get started on doing something that may have seemed impossible, such as starting a business. I often have conversations with average people, like myself, who dream of starting a business but seem to allow less-than-ideal conditions to stand in their way. My hope is that by reading this book, these same people will be able to overcome these mental obstacles and realize that they are more than capable of establishing a successful business despite what their surroundings may look like. As you'll soon learn throughout these pages, the internet changed everything and can therefore cost you next to nothing to get started on a business right now.

This book is divided into three parts. The first part covers more of the mental side of starting a business, by highlighting specific areas of early entrepreneurship that can better prepare you for your journey along the way. The second part discusses things that will need to be done in order to establish the basics of your business. The third part demonstrates aspects of a startup once it is officially open to the market, namely, ways in which to keep your momentum moving and your business growing.

Oh and one last tidbit, notice the size of the book. It's small for your benefit, because I'd much rather you spend your time getting started on your business than reading this book all day. So, as I would say to my friends, stop procrastinating and let's get to work!

"When there is a hill to climb, don't think that waiting will make it smaller."

~Anonymous

PART I
THE MIND

~The Power of Getting Started~

Be honest. How many times have you wanted to start your own business, but never did because you allowed the fear of failure, judgment or rejection to stop you before you even started? If I'm being honest I've done it myself, which is one of the reasons why I wrote this book in the first place. The question of *why* we do it isn't as important as *how* do we change it? Thankfully, there's a book for that, and you happen to be reading it right now.

The decision to start a business is a delicate one. Much is to be considered, and it can leave you feeling intimidated, but the actual power to overcome these mental obstacles really lies in the act of getting started. Whatever your motivating factors are for wanting to start a business, one thing is for certain: each day that passes is an opportunity to make it happen. For me, the deciding factor was having to digest the reality of a very sobering quote by motivational speaker Tony Gaskins who boldly stated "If you don't build your dream someone will hire you to build theirs." After much reflection I came to the conclusion that the difference between doing one or the other is the willingness to take the first step. Will it be difficult? Most likely. Will you want to quit? At times, probably.

But also keep in mind that NOTHING in the history of mankind has ever been achieved without someone taking that first step. So will it be worth it? Without a doubt.

~The Perks of Dream Chasing~

This topic is important, and I want to share my reasoning on why I included it. If you want to do anything big in life, you must first start small. This is not just true in business, but in nature, as well. For example, which do you think would be easier, planting an oak tree or planting the seed of an oak tree? Most would argue the latter, including myself. Nothing starts out massive and we should approach our goals in the same manner. There may be times when you lose sight of why you are chasing your dream of starting a business, and when that happens, remember the added benefits that come along with doing so:

1.   **It gives you direction--**When you know where you're headed, chances are, you're going to get there. If ever you feel overwhelmed, remember where you are ultimately trying to go. As long as you keep your eyes on the prize, an occasional bump-in-the-road or setback won't deter you from reaching your destination.

2.   **It improves your focus--**It's easy to get sidetracked by all that life has to offer. Having a goal helps keep the most important things right in front of you. When times like these occur, remember *why* you are doing it, and remember the people you are doing it for.

3.   It provides a purpose--Sometimes we all feel like giving up at one time or another, especially when other aspects of our life aren't in a good place. Pursuing your goal can give you reason to press on and keep going. I, personally, benefited from this aspect, as during the early stages of building SmartPhoneRecords, my father passed away and left me devastated for many months. Having a purpose undoubtedly helped me to stay the course, focus on my mission and begin to heal all at the same time.

It's no coincidence the aforementioned dream-chasing perks can be used interchangeably. Allow them to help guide you to your ultimate destination. Remember that starting small allows more room for understanding of the process, which in turn will help create a successful business.

~Permission Slip~

This is something I'm willing to bet we've all done at some point in our lives and it could be the demise of your business before it even gets started if you aren't aware that you do it.

There are a couple of ways to interpret this. One is coming from the angle of family, friends and even co-workers. To be honest, most of those around you will not understand why you want to start your own business. Some may even try and talk you out of it. That's because they are the ones busy helping other people build their dreams. Remember them? This is where the term "permission slip" comes in. You may not get validation from those you love and interact with, so prepare yourself in the event permission is what you seek. To be fair, starting a business is risky and definitely not for the faint of heart. If it were easy, everyone would be doing it. But don't let that deter you from your mission. It can be done.

The other angle is waiting for approval from professionals. Many people think they need validation from "experts" in order to move forward with their goals. For example, when writing this book, I didn't need permission from a publisher, nor did I spend my time studying literature in order to get consent to do it. I simply wanted to share my insight with those who might be able to use it, and so I did. The reality is, you having a dream and a clear vision of how to obtain it is permission enough. There may come a time during the process that you'll need a professional to give their input, but certainly not to give their blessing on your dream to start a business.

~Stay Out of the Convincing Business~

Here's a concept that I have found to be extremely useful while building my startup. The hard truth is that not everyone is going to be as enthusiastic as you are about your product. Everything isn't for everyone and that's okay. Instead of taking it personal, use these moments as opportunities to focus on those who like what you're doing and not the ones who don't. Look at it this way, why date someone if you have to convince them to be with you? Chances are, you'll probably have to convince them to *stay* with you, which, in the long run, may turn out to be more work than it's worth. Ultimately, your best bet is to be open to push-back but don't allow it to slow down your marketing objective. There will be plenty of people who'll want what you're selling.

~Forget About the Time Factor~

Don't focus on the amount of time it may take to get your business up and running. Whether you start today, tomorrow, or two years from now, the time will pass anyway. I think the late Jim Rohn put it best when he said, "Ten years from now you will surely arrive. The question is, where?" Again, the key here is to just get started. Even if time is not available in abundance, a little bit every day will make a difference. The amount of time it takes you to complete any task is a direct result of the amount of work put in.

~Ambition Broadcasting~

It's common practice these days for us human beings to share just about any and all information with everyone, especially when having social media right at our fingertips. But when it comes to your personal goals, specifically, starting a business, letting others know about your ambitions too soon can be more counterproductive than you may think. Here are three points to consider:

1.   **Give yourself some time for your idea to mature and develop--**Thoroughly think it through on your own, first. Take some time to collect as many pros and cons as you can, as well as back-up plans, in the event things don't go as you had originally intended. Things happen. Additionally, having these answers will

come in handy when discussing your ideas with those who will be affected by your decision.

2. Beware of those with negative dispositions--While people may have good intentions, telling others what you are *thinking about doing* only opens the door for them to try and persuade you to change your mind. That's why allowing your idea to mature in your mind is so important; when the neigh-sayers start to tell you all the reasons it won't work, you'll have comfort in knowing all the reasons why it will.

3. Take advantage of the head-start--You'll need time for due-diligence. This is when doing extensive research is most important. Investigate the current industry of your business. Also, what is its history and who will be your competitors? What are some of the things that you will absolutely have to have in order to get your business off the ground?

There will always be time to introduce your idea to the world. Avoid getting caught up in the whirlwind of sharing too prematurely and spend that time working on transforming your idea into a functioning business instead. Besides, the more you're "broadcasting," the less you're working.

~Adopt a Philosophy, or Two~

Why does this matter? Well, doing so will help keep things in perspective when you need it most. Perspective is a powerful weapon and has a profound impact on how we view the world, our lives, each other, and ourselves. What makes it so powerful is the ability it gives us to choose between two types--positive and negative--and centering around either one will be the difference between quitting and seeing something through. Here are five that I greatly leaned on during my startup process:

1. Your Attitude Determines Your Altitude--This is not a new concept but it is absolutely true. No matter what you go through or pursue in life, approaching it with a positive mentality will always lead to positive results. Successful people are not without problems, they just figure out how to solve or work through them. If you are ever in need of philosophical ideology as I was at times, be proactive and search for them. The internet is a fast and effective instrument to find inspiration. I often listened to YouTube clips featuring popular motivational speakers to help combat any negative energy I was feeling, namely, Les Brown, Jim Rohn, Napoleon Hill, Tony Robbins and Dr. Eric Thomas. Of course, there are a number of other great speakers to choose from, so take some time to find the ones whose messages resonate with you.

2. Begin with the End in Mind--Think of how a house is built. Before any work is started a blueprint of what it should look like is always drafted. In order to draft the blueprint, a vision of the house had to first be designed in someone's mind. Simply put, the clearer the vision, the more likely you are to obtain it. This mindset can even be applied to your daily life. Visualize what you'd like to accomplish by the end of each day and set out to make it happen. You may not always get it all done, but the idea is that doing so day after day will eventually lead you and your business to long-term success. What does your business "end" look like?

3.   Nature is Neutral--You know the saying, "Love is Blind"? So is nature, especially when it comes to starting your business. While it's true that the proverbial glass ceiling still exists on many fronts, it's now much easier to break through with the advancements of both the internet and smartphones. Nature doesn't care what you look like, where you've been or where you're going. As long as you put in the work, you will get the results you're looking for, and anything one person can accomplish, so can you.

4.   Exercise the Law of Averages--If you're not familiar with how it works, it's basically the notion that the more a particular task is performed the better the odds are at succeeding. More than anything, this concept helps prepare me for rejection. Why would I do that? One, rejection is inevitable and two, it's really not as bad as we make it out to be. Do you recall earlier when I mentioned how not everything is for everyone? This is where the **Law of Averages** comes in handy. You may not always win them over. But the more you keep working, pursuing, reaching out and sharing what you're doing, the chances of you piquing the interest of potential customers, as well as investors dramatically increase. It also helps during the times of anxiousness when you feel as if things aren't progressing fast enough. Things take time, and starting a business is no exception.

5.   You Never Know--It's true. You just never know what may happen by taking   a chance on yourself. I tend to lean on this one whenever I embark on a journey down an unbeaten path. Initially I grapple with the fear of failing, talking myself in and then right back out of whatever it is I'm contemplating on doing. But having this mindset helps get me through my trepidation and any subsequent lingering doubt. Although it may seem unsophisticated, it is effective.

~Pull Inspiration From Everywhere~

It's a great feeling to be an expert at something, to know how it is supposed to function from beginning to end and to master its intricacies. But even this has its disadvantages. Once you reach such a threshold, especially when it comes to your business, it's good to educate yourself on how other businesses operate and thrive. Take Henry Ford, for example. He built his vast fortune mass-producing automobiles by way of assembly line after being inspired by learning how a meat-packing company processed its inventory. Ironically, Detroit native and Motown Records founder Barry Gordy, who once worked on these same Ford assembly lines, implemented this ingenuity to help generate massive success for his company by piecing together various creative teams designed to help catapult his artists to the top of the music charts. Allow yourself to be a novice whenever possible, as doing so can help transcend your business in ways you didn't know were possible.

~Embrace the Downsides~

Yes, there are "downsides." But again, perspective is key. Each startup has its boring moments, mundane tasks, and in its infancy, can't be left unattended for very long. Determining what is "boring" or "mundane" is contingent upon your likes and dislikes, be it making phone calls, spending time on social media, doing research, etc. But even these unpleasant attributes of starting a business serve a bigger purpose and are extremely necessary.

Additionally, if not more importantly, another downside is how entrepreneurship can affect your social life and personal relationships. This was something I wasn't aware of, nor prepared for when I set out to form SmartPhoneRecords. There have been countless birthdays, holidays, celebrations and other special events that I have had to miss due to the demands of these downsides. Many times I have had to cancel or reschedule plans, or turn myself off from the rest of the world in order to do what needed to be done. Relationships with your friends, loved ones and even your social life may sometimes suffer, but know that not only is making such sacrifices vital to the success of your business, but that times like these are only temporary.

~Finish What You Start~

There is much to be said about a person who finishes what they start. Anyone can have great intentions and legitimate aspirations, but only those with great determination see them through to the end. I think that's why a college education is so appreciated and required within today's workforce. It's really not about the "piece of paper" that comes with it, but rather the accomplishment of not giving up. With that said, imagine the number of groundbreaking ideas that were never realized because their owners abandoned them too soon. Think of all lives that could have been emphatically changed if these same people decided to finish what their imagination started.

We each have a natural tendency to doubt or underestimate our own abilities. Giving up is such an easy thing to do, especially when a perfectly-suited excuse is lurking around every corner, but don't allow it to be an option. Fulfilling your desire to start a business will not only be rewarding, but will be a part of the legacy you leave behind for your loved ones. After all, if you don't believe in yourself, no one else will, and rightfully so.

"I always say the first sign of a good idea
is a lot of people not believing in it. I can
tell you this right now, if you have an
idea that makes complete logical sense
and people don't believe in it, then
you probably have a brilliant idea."

~Steve Stoute

PART II
THE BUSINESS

~Exploring Ideas~

Doesn't it seem like just when all the "good" ideas are already taken, BAM!--something comes along that causes you to say "Damn. How come I didn't think of that?" Why do such inventions leave us asking this question? My hunch is that more often than not we assume that such ideas are so good or so obvious that someone must already be in the process of developing them. That, or when we do think of a great idea, it ends up getting left behind due to the overwhelming feeling of not knowing where to start or even how to begin. It really doesn't have to be this way. The good news is that we have the Internet which has the ability to provide us with just about any type of information we are looking for. This is a fast and simple way to determine if someone is already working on something you want to create. Technology has allowed almost everyone to be accessible, largely being those who own and operate a business. The chances of someone else working on the very same idea and there not be any record of it are slim.

According to the Small Business Administration (SBA), 543,000 new businesses are started every month. Depending on how you view it, you either feel relieved by this or intimidated. I view it as a positive thing. This number should serve as a reminder that there's clearly enough room for you and your startup. If you know what type of business you want to go into, this is great news. But if you aren't sure, that is okay, too. Although the purpose of this book isn't to tell you what business to start, I've listed a few options to examine if you're seriously considering business ownership but don't know exactly which one:

1.   You Don't Need to Reinvent the Wheel --Your idea doesn't have to be an original one for it to be successful. Originality and creativity are two completely different things. Products ranging from household goods to the automotive industry are constantly being modified and upgraded everyday. Is there an existing business or service currently on the market that you think you could improve upon? Perhaps there is a specific demographic that you can reach that other companies won't target.

2.   Hobbies and Natural Talents--A hobby is a great place to focus on as these are done out of pleasure and at your leisure. They say that if you do what you love, you'll never work a day in your life, so taking a closer look into the things that you enjoy doing will be worth the time spent. Just like originality and creativity, hobbies and talent are not one in the same. They can be, but not always are they synonymous. What are your natural abilities? Writing? Gardening? Cooking? Public Speaking? Regardless of what it is, don't take it lightly because what you possess as a talent can be a struggle for the next person, and most likely, thousands, even millions more. These are the people who'll become your customers.

3.   Scratch Your Own Itch--What bothers you? Do you have a need for something that no one on the market seems to be addressing? More than likely, if you have an issue with it, many others do, too. By creating a business that focuses on solving your own problem, you just may end up solving it for millions of others at the same time.

The message here is to allow yourself permission to consider all possibilities. Give your mind the freedom to think "outside" the box because doing so will only expand your creativity. Also, don't allow other factors such as what other companies have done or are doing to deter you from anything you may be considering. As an example, the idea for SmartPhoneRecords really presented itself when I saw there was a need for a more convenient process of distributing the music I made. Sure, there were plenty of platforms available that did the job but they also required certain equipment that I didn't own, namely, a PC. What I did have, however, was a smartphone. So after much extensive, painstaking research I found my answer: I was going to create a business that allowed music artists to upload and sell their music using only their smartphone. It wasn't that I necessarily expected everyone to like it or to even use it but I knew that if the current methods of music distribution were a problem for me, they were a problem for others, as well. My point is that I didn't waste any time debating about why these same platforms didn't offer such a feature, nor did I sit idle assuming that they were out there somewhere in the process of creating it. The need for it was evident and that was good enough for me.

~Establish a Digital Footprint~

There has never been a better time than right now to become an entrepreneur. Whether you realize it or not, every business now has the ability to reach people all over the globe. With the World Wide Web at our fingertips, even businesses with physical locations have the potential to acquire a vast number of customers that would have been unreachable at any other time in history. Of course, in order to be a part of it, you'll need to establish your own website, as having one instantly puts you in a position to advertise to billions of people around the world at any given moment. I'll explain more in the next several paragraphs.

~Cheaper Ways To Finance Your Business~

There's a saying that goes "it takes money to make money." Well, I disagree. In fact, the purpose of this section is to show you ways that can help you to at least get the basics you'll need without having to spend a boatload of money.

In my opinion, what's worth more than money today is ingenuity and creativity, and it's also the person who relentlessly refuses to accept failure and uses what they have to reach their goal. The fact of the matter is that you really don't need a big office or to hire a bunch of people, and you certainly don't need to drain your bank account in order to make it happen. As long as you own either a computer or a smartphone, you have everything you need to start your business.

For starters, your smartphone is an exceptional tool to utilize for many things besides texting. With the advancement of handheld devices, most, if not all, camera phones provide high definition resolution, endless filters, video capabilities, and editing options, to name a few. This can help to market your product, and with promotional campaigns when it's time to bring attention to your business, all without spending a dime (other than the monthly phone bill you already pay for). This is just one example. Where you lack in money, make up for in creativity.

Below are some options you may want to look into to get things done on a budget. I am not being paid nor sponsored to mention these companies or methods, they are simply services that, as an entrepreneur, I found helpful when I was building SmartPhoneRecords. Hopefully you'll find them to be just as useful if you happen to be in a similar financial situation that I was in at the time. Feel free to do your own research on these companies and/or terms, and remember that there are many other resources out there that I have yet to discover, so be sure to take some time to find out which options best fit your needs:

Legalzoom.com -- This is a platform that helps you establish your business with whatever state you live in. It's very user-friendly and will also help you keep track of important compliance dates along the way by sending you notification reminders.

Mynewcompany.com -- Another website to register and establish your company for sometimes as low as $79.

GoogleVoice.com -- A service that can provide your business with an alternative phone number in order to keep your personal number private. This call forwarding service also allows for personalized or "vanity" numbers which are great for business. Oh, and it's free.

RingCentral.com -- This company, for a small fee, assigns you a "1-800" number for your business, including separate extensions for your team members.

Interns -- Great to have because they provide new energy and ideas and want to build their résumés at the same time.

Outsourcing -- Work or production overseas can come with its own challenges but if the proper due diligence is done on your part, you can save a ton of money for early stage manufacturing or technical jobs.

Fiverr.com -- An awesome service for getting jobs completed for only $5.

Hiring Ads -- I believe there to be a little reverse psychology that comes into play when running hiring ads. When you need something done and people compete for the job, the prices drop. Try it!

PRlog.com & PR.com -- Tell the world about your company yourself. Write your own press release and post it for free on one of these sites. They also have paid features to expand your reach for further distribution.

Bluehost.com -- Free website domain and hosting for as low as $3.95/month.

GoDaddy.com -- Another free website with domain and hosting options.

"F.I.T." Program -- Better known as Facebook, Instagram and Twitter - free social medial sites to connect with millions around the world.

Graphio -- A free mobile app that's user friendly and great for creating ads and diagrams.

Backpage.com and Craigslist.com -- Free global online classifieds website.

Forums -- Online forums are useful for building awareness for your company and finding niche crowds.

Meetup.com -- Not a dating website, but rather a platform that helps connect you with like-minded professionals that you may potentially be able to learn from or partner with in order to facilitate your startup needs.

Virtual offices -- These are designed to give you a place to house your business at a fraction of the buying or rental cost. For a monthly fee, a "virtual office" allows you to set up shop by providing you phone answering services, a business address and conference rooms when needed, thus alleviating the privacy and personal security concerns that can arise when running a home-based business.

Keep in mind that the climate of business nowadays has changed. There is no longer a requirement for new companies to appear big and corporate-like anymore. In fact, it's almost the complete opposite. People are becoming more accepting and attracted to the independent vendor versus large companies because the customer experience and quality is usually better and the prices are lower due to a smaller overhead. It's quite alright to be a small business in a big world. If your company is just you or two of you, don't be afraid to be upfront about it. Have faith in your product or service by letting your customers know, and you just may be surprised at how many customers appreciate your candor.

~The Octopus~

One way to scale your business is to treat it as though it were an octopus, a soft-bodied sea creature that has eight long limbs protruding from its round head. Visualize your business as the head of the body, while each limb represents a specific aspect of your business that can be individualized and even monetized. Let's use a personal training startup as an example. The actual personal trainer, in this case, you, represents the head of the octopus and the limbs reflect the various areas of skills you possess. It may look something like this:

1. **Exercising--** Create various programs for different body types and ages by combining both cardiovascular and weight-resistance workouts. Share before and after results.

2. **Classes--** Set up a "virtual" classroom. This can be especially helpful to those who may not have the time or money to put into an actual gym membership.

3. **Education--** Start a blog. This is where you can connect with your customers on a personal level. Share with them who you are and how working out has shaped your life. You can also highlight the progress of clients who have benefited from following your guidelines, and include all of the benefits of maintaining a healthy lifestyle.

4. **Supplements--** Become an expert on the extensive vitamins and supplements market.

5.   Meal Plans-- Create personalized meal plans for customers tailored to their specific goals.

6.   Q&As-- Set up weekly Skype calls or online chat sessions for those who seek fitness information.

7.   Nutrition-- Help your clients to learn how nutrition effects their health.

8.   Branding-- Take all of the above and put it under one umbrella, so to speak, and turn it into a business of itself. This can stretch your revenue far beyond the scope of solely training your clients in a gym setting.

Keep in mind that it's not absolutely necessary to have eight "limbs." Some may only have four, while others may have 14, but eight is a good number to target. Regardless of how many you are able to come up with for your specific business, the important thing is to find ways to market yourself. The more ways you have to sell your business, the more customers you'll attract.

~Research~

Doing extensive market research on the industry you are planning to enter is crucial. I've read somewhere before that you should never ask a question you haven't asked Google first. With a quick Google search you can find out just about anything you need to know on any field, such as videos, statistical information, and historical data, to name a few. Keep in mind that doing research is more like a marathon than a sprint. Each market performs differently, and all are constantly changing and evolving. Below I've listed three areas to consider while doing your research to help get you started:

1. Who will your customers be? Who are the people that have a need for your product or service?

2. Who will be your competitors? What other businesses, if any, are already doing what you plan on doing?

3. Market Size -- What does the local, national and global market look like?

It's also a good idea to check the websites of your local Chamber of Commerce, the Small Business Administration and the U.S. Census Bureau. The more research you do, the better you'll be able to understand the market, and in turn, better serve your future customers.

~Competitors~

When analyzing your competition it's important to pay attention not only to things like business models, and marketing strategies, but it's a good idea to look at how they began, as well. Who are the founders and why did they start these companies in the first place? Find out their stories. Learning about your competition isn't just studying what they do and how big they are, it's about knowing their backstory and their purpose. This will help when you start thinking about how to build your business and market it in a way that separates you from the rest.

Furthermore, people tend to view competition in a negative fashion, as if there's only enough room in the world for one or two of the same thing. Imagine only one type of car, or clothing brand or wine. Don't fall victim to this mentality. Competition is supposed to bring out the best in opponents and to push the culture of an industry forward. So long as you aren't infringing upon a competitor's copyright or patent, there's always room for a new company who's willing to bring something different to the table.

That said, it's also important to look at the things you like about your competition. What are some methods they use that you might be able to implement on a smaller scale? Remember that if your competition is a big company, they are large for a reason and didn't get there by doing all the wrong things.

~"Burn to Learn"~

If there's one thing I've learned as an entrepreneur, it's that you don't have to experience every situation firsthand in order to learn from one. When you first start out as your own boss, there are many things that you'll figure out along the way. However, if you have the opportunity to absorb the lessons learned by those who've gone before you, do not pass it up. I recommend spending some time learning about how other people in your field either failed or became successful. Biographies are a great source for stories of triumphs and adversity. Also, don't be afraid to seek out a mentor or someone who is doing what you'd like to do.The wealth of knowledge you could potentially gain just may be the difference between your business failing or succeeding.

~Paint a Picture~

At some point, you're going to have to explain what your business is, and not just once, but over and over. That's why it's good to have a tagline that can sum up what your startup is about, especially if what you're doing has never been done before.

"Painting a picture" is more than just a tagline. It needs to be able to give people a mental description of who and what you are. This will take both time and brainstorming. First, you'll want to write down your idea and as many details as you can think of. Doing this will help you to keep things organized and give you a clearer vision of what your business will look like overall. This is an important step that you mustn't skip, because it will help you create the one thing that is a must when establishing your startup: its culture. Business culture is like an evolving backdrop. It sets the tone for what a company stands for, encompassing its values, beliefs and moral principles. The idea here is to establish absolute clarity for your audience. The easier it is for them to understand, the likelier they'll want to be a part of what you're doing.

~Teaming Up~

The hardest part about running any business is finding good people to work with. There are numerous factors that can make or break a startup striving to get off the ground, but nothing will slow the process down faster than a bunch of fucking dickheads. I think author Napoleon Hill put it best when he declared "To get people to work together in the spirit of harmony is one of the greatest human achievements."

A time will come when you'll need to enlist the help of another person or company to help further your progress. My first and foremost piece of advice is to protect yourself by doing your due diligence. Take the time to find out about the people you are considering doing business with. This should include how long they've been in business, if they're registered with the Better Business Bureau (BBB), online reviews, and don't be afraid of inquiring about references from past clients.

If, after you've done your due diligence, you wish to continue doing business with this person (or company), remember that you can always give them a smaller job to start with before committing yourself to any long-term agreement. This will give you the opportunity not only to see how well they perform but how well you work together. In the event you're ready to take the next step, it's a good idea that both parties discuss what their expectations are of one another. Where do each of you stand when it comes to how you conduct business? What do each of you hope to achieve by working with one another? What do you require from each other that must be understood before moving forward? What is important to you--Punctuality? Work Ethic? Reliability? Communication? These are precisely the things that should be clarified prior to entering into any lengthy contract or partnership. The important thing is communication. Once these guidelines are established, the likelihood of reoccurring misunderstandings should lessen substantially, if not completely. Lastly, I highly encourage you to consider the following to best combat any confusion:

1. Have a written contract--Ensure it states the responsibilities of all persons involved and what is expected of them.

2. Set goal deadlines--This will confirm specific dates of when said goals should be completed. It'll also make certain everyone is on the same page about what is due and when.

3. Document as you go--I cannot stress this enough. Keep ALL emails, text messages, and any other means of communication. If you are using other software applications, such as mobile apps to communicate, take screen shots of all exchanges between you and the other party. Conference calls and webcam sessions should be well documented, noting the date and time, and what was discussed.

Remember, you are responsible for protecting yourself. If you don't, you won't be in a position to protect your business or those you love and provide for.

~Prototypes and Business Models~

Before you bring your product or service to market, a few things will need to be done first. Specifically, if you have a physical product, creating a **prototype**, or "preliminary mockup" is not only necessary for showing people how it works, but more importantly, to find out IF it works. This is how you will determine if what you created in your mind reflects its real life functionality. If it doesn't, this is the time to make adjustments. Because each industry is different, each prototype will be, too. Include in your research how to go about developing one for the market you are looking to become a part of.

If your business provides a service rather than an actual product, you will still need a way to show how it works. This is where a demonstration, or "demo" is useful. Again, how you arrange yours will be determined by the industry your service belongs to.

Up next, you'll need a **business model**. According to Investopedia.com, this is defined as "the plan implemented by a company to generate revenue and make a profit from operations." In other words, what are all the ways that you plan on making money? Keep in mind that this is where you'll detail the intricacies of your plan, as that is the key word, here. For instance, how will your business make money? Do you need partners, distributors or salespeople in order to operate? Will you need a physical location and rent an office space or will you work from home? These are just a few specifics that you will need to include in your business model, though it will likely change as time passes and your business grows. Nevertheless, knowing how your business will generate revenue and operate on a daily basis is essential because a company without a business model is equivalent to playing a game without rules or instruction, and can quickly turn into a disorganized mess.

There are a plethora of websites online to help get you started in the right direction when tackling this portion of your startup journey. Since each business will require different prototypes and business models, take some time to discover which ones will be appropriate for your startup needs.

~Start With You, First~

I once read about a 19 year old kid who started a business and raised $20 million dollars from investors to finance it. By the time he was 21, the money was gone, he was bankrupt and his business folded. I imagine that your reaction just now was one of utter disbelief or frustration, or perhaps even both and everything in between. My point is, sometimes having too much can cause problems instead of fix them. Depending on the kind of business you plan on building, it's best to do as much as you possibly can on your own before enlisting the help of anyone else. The most rewarding part of self-starting is that you learn about every aspect of your business down to the most infinitesimal detail. And the more you understand how it works on these levels, the more confidence you'll have in making future decisions down the road. After all, no one should ever know more than you do about *your* business.

Don't watch the clock;
do what it does.

Keep Going

~Sam Levenson

PART III

The Launch

There have been many people throughout history that have worked tirelessly to make it to the top, only to fall off because they failed to manage the heights and responsibilities that came along with it. In this last section, I'll share with you some thoughts to consider once your business is live and fully functioning, as well as things that can be helpful in order to help keep your business afloat thereafter.

~Don't Kill Your Momentum~

The actual launching of a business is a very significant milestone for an entrepreneur. It's the day you introduce to the world what you have created, reflecting many days of hard work, sacrifice, and dedication. It also proves that you can execute a plan to the end. And while all of this will be an exciting time for you, don't forget that your job is not over. In fact, it is just beginning. That is why I strongly urge you not to allow this period of celebration to kill the momentum you've built thus far. It may get tempting to want to take a break and bask in your accomplishment, but this will be the time where, believe it or not, you will need to hustle even harder than before. Now is when you will need to start building your customer base, and how you acquire and keep these customers will determine your success. Don't take the momentum you've built up to this point for granted because for one, you've worked incredibly hard to get it and two, once you lose it, it will not be easy to get it back. Below, I've listed some ways to help keep it moving in the right direction:

1. Social Media and Blogging--Popular websites and mobile apps are great for finding customers around the globe. Social media, especially, has given a whole new meaning to the term "word of mouth." Whether you use it or not, when it comes to your startup, social media is your best friend! This is one of the reasons I insist that it is easier now than ever before to start a business. It's basically a free advertising agency. Think about it: using social media saves you an abundance of time and money. Where people used to have to travel and constantly be on the road knocking on doors to promote their product, now all you have to do is get on your smartphone or nearest computer to do the very same thing. Before social media, business owners would have no choice but to spend hundreds or thousands of dollars advertising via television, radio stations, newspapers and magazines. Not only that, but the demographic of the receiving audience may not have been who they intended to target in the first place. Simply put, social media has given business owners the gift of more time, energy and money. And who wouldn't want that?

Blogging is another helpful tool. Use it to share information as well as to share your story, too. This is a great way to connect more personally with your customers, and to build a rapport with them along the way. Blogging is also convenient in that it can be done at your leisure, or on a daily, weekly or monthly basis.

2. Partnerships--Collaborating with an existing company is beneficial for you as it expands your network of people and resources. It can also help you to learn about another business and/or industry that you would otherwise not know about, possibly inspiring you to implement procedures of theirs into your own practice.

3. Affiliate Programs--This is, in a nutshell, a referral strategy. By creating an affiliate program, your existing customers assist by helping build your customer base in return for perks provided by your company. For instance, when our affiliate customers at SPR give a non-customer a certain code (provided to them by our company), the affiliate is then rewarded with a percentage of that new customer's earnings every time their material is sold within our app. One thing to keep in mind, your affiliates don't necessarily have to be customers in order for either of you to benefit from this program.

4. Online Advertising--Free websites such as Craigslist.org and Backpage.com pull in millions of users in daily traffic. Creating a few ads with your website information can help attract a significant amount of people to your business. Don't knock it 'til you try it, by the way.

5. Conventions and Trade Shows--These are industry specific and most likely have many dedicated to your line of work. They can be extremely helpful in acquiring new patrons, and afford you the opportunity to network with companies in your industry, professionals in other industries, possible investors and even media personnel. Events like these are often attended by thousands of members of the public who pay to browse at the latest upcoming startups within a specific industry, exposing you to many new potential new customers. Search for trade shows in your area to find out if you qualify for a free booth to promote your startup.

6. Traditional Advertising--Examples include: television, billboards, radio, magazines, bus stops, etc. Although these are the most expensive forms of advertising on this list, I felt it necessary to include them anyway. If and when you have the money to use these outlets, they will definitely aid in driving business in your direction, but don't feel obligated to use them if you're not in the financial position to do so.

7. Press Releases--You don't have to wait for someone else to write about you. Tell your own story and publish it on a website designed specifically for releasing written content directed at the public and members of the media. Websites like Free-Press-Release.com and PR.com allow you to put your business in the spotlight before millions of people all over the world. Prices range from free to premium services, depending on what you are able to afford.

8. Hook Models--These are loyalty programs, buy-one-get-one offers, special discounts, etc., that serve as rewards for returning customers. More importantly, hook models can also just be a kick-ass product with outstanding customer service that makes your customers come back for more. Going above and beyond for your customers can produce many benefits. Not only do they help finance your business, but their commitment to your company can help with gaining leverage that can eventually separate you from your competition.

~Feedback~

Now that you've launched and are officially on the market, feedback, whether welcomed or otherwise, will start to trickle in. Take this opportunity to learn how you can improve your service or product, but remember that you will not be able to please everyone. Just as I previously mentioned, you won't win everyone over, and that is okay. Listen intently to those taking the time to give their opinion but also don't feel the need to run out and change everything that was suggested to you, either. No one likes to hear negative feedback, but don't take it personal if you find someone who thinks your "baby" is unattractive. This is part of being an entrepreneur. The great part about feedback is that it is free advice. Take what applies, and let the rest fly. Be sure your customers know where they can turn if they do have questions, complaints or suggestions, whether it be in email form, through your website, a suggestion box or even a survey. Feedback is essential and should be used as a guideline to gauge whether what you are doing is effective or needs some adjusting.

~Staying Small~

There is this school of thought in the business world today, primarily the tech industry, that you are supposed to grow a company as fast as possible and then turn around and sell it. Before I became familiar with the world of startups I would often hear of these stories and wonder why anyone would put in all the work it requires to start a business, just to turn around and sell it. Eventually it dawned on me that the people who were actually teaching this "growth school" method were often people who were not founders of companies, themselves, but investors. Investors love to push this business strategy onto startups, because that is when investors get paid. Don't feel pressured to fall into this trap just for the sake of growth, itself. Don't be afraid to stay small until you to learn the nature of the business you're in. There will be things you won't initially know how to do, but having a good grasp on all phases of your business will only help you to create a better product or service.

~Take Advantage of Being a Startup~

A startup is considered to be a business less than five years old. This means that they have an advantage that businesses older than this time frame do not. There are a number of opportunities to take advantage of during your startup years that are put in place to help take it to the next level. One opportunity to look into is applying for incubators. An incubator, in terms of business, is a company or organization designed to help accelerate the growth and subsequent success of startups by providing them a variety of support systems that would otherwise be difficult for a budding entrepreneur to access. Such support may include (but are not limited to) locating a physical space, capital, coaching, mentorship and networking with other business leaders and investors. Every incubator runs differently, but usually lasts between three to six months with a small investment made to the startup in exchange for a percentage of ownership in the company. Incubators are structured like academic courses with curriculum that is followed throughout the entire program, concluding with a "demo" day where you present your product or service to investors, mentors and the public.

~Beware of Startup Scams~

The harsh reality is that not everyone is going to have your best interest in mind. There are some people who will do anything for money no matter the damage they cause, which is why I want to remind you that all money isn't good money. It's tempting to want to put your faith in someone who seems to have all the answers to success, but understand that thinking logically is a must when these wolves in sheep's clothing appear. My rule of thumb--if it sounds too good to be true, it probably is. Here are a couple of things I want you to know:

I don't care what anyone tells you. If someone is charging you money to pitch to investors, it is a scam! This is not how legitimate agencies and credible businesses operate. Think logically for a moment--why would a struggling startup need to spend what little money they do have just to meet with people who have all the money in the first place? It doesn't make any sense. Real investors won't charge you anything to hear what you have to say. They understand that they make money *after* the investment is made and no sooner. Don't get so caught up in empty promises that you forget to think logically about the situation. No one will protect you the way you protect yourself!

Also, just because someone offers you money or a deal of some kind, doesn't mean you have to take it. If you are approached with an offer, keep these things in mind:

1. You don't have to rush. This is one of the oldest tricks in the business book. When someone is pressuring you to sign a contract, make sure you don't trip over the big red flag as you run out the door. Any deal worth making is worth doing right and thoroughly. And any decent business person understands this and welcomes you taking time to ensure such a deal is in your best interest.

2. Lawyer up. Don't use the legal representation of the same person with whom you are dealing business. Again, any legitimate professional will already know this and would not conduct their business in this manner.   Be sure to find a reputable lawyer to represent you so that you understand everything about the proposal from start to finish. He or she will be able to help you sift through any documents that are presented and can help you decide if signing the contract is the right thing to do.

3. Ask questions. Who are they and what is there background? How many companies have they invested in? Are they legally allowed to be engaging in such negotiations? What will their role be when it comes to your business, and how involved will they be? Are they just providing capital or do they also have connections and resources available to you? How much control of your company do they want in exchange for their financial backing?

Knowing these answers can save you a tremendous amount of time and money and is also another way of protecting yourself and your business. Be proactive.

~Put Yourself in a Position to be Chosen~

Not many people know that they can apply to be nominated for awards within their industry. I view these as a win-win situation, as well as another opportunity to promote your business. Entering your company in contests helps on a number of levels. Specifically:

1. It helps to see where your business stands in the eyes of your industry. All competitions have guidelines that must be met in order to be considered. Knowing what these guidelines consist of can help you determine what still needs to be done. For example, does your business need to be "incorporated?" Are there a certain number of customers, or social media presence/popularity level that must be reached first? Does the competition require that you have a certain amount of team members? These, along with several other criterion are instrumental in ensuring your business is ready to compete with the best in your field.

2. You may get the chance to receive professional feedback. This is a great opportunity to get the opinions of true professionals in your industry. Sometimes when you are not chosen to be shortlisted for an award, feedback is provided to help you better understand why you were not selected. Embrace this opportunity to absorb as much feedback as possible so that you can make the necessary adjustments where suggested.

3. If you are nominated, it proves you are on par with your industry's standards. Not only have you met the requirements to compete but your company has been recognized for its excellence among your peers. This acknowledgment will be something you can be proud of for the remainder of your entrepreneurship.

4. Winning never hurts. This is proof that your hard work and dedication is commended and recognized within your professional community, and is also an accomplishment that you can associate with your future business endeavors.

~Closing~

In closing, starting a business is not about what you get, but rather what you become. When pursuing a goal in life, it's natural to only focus on the end result or what we plan to have once we finally reach it. While on your startup journey, don't lose sight of the person you are becoming while in the process. How have you changed? What do you know now that you didn't before? What are some things you have discovered about yourself and those around you? In what ways are you growing? These questions are important to answer, because they help you to appreciate how far you've come and maybe even how much further you need to go. Let them be reminders that we are all in progress of some sort. How you handle the various challenges that come with being an entrepreneur is going to be what separates the live from the jive. The amount of research, discipline and even rejection can be enough to make some people want to give up and quit. But even these feelings of uncertainty can be overcome by anyone who's willing to keep going and see it through. When we extract the lessons learned from the challenges we face, we gain the personal growth, wisdom and the ability to persevere through a life that truly reflects what we're worth and how far we've come. Reaching our goal is just the icing on the cake.

Thanks for reading.

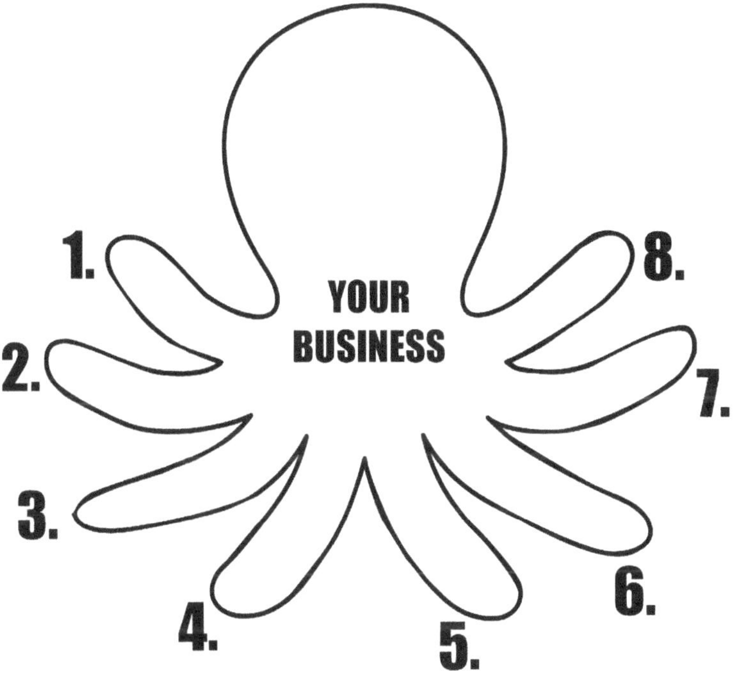

SHUT UP AND
STARTUP
IDEAS AND NOTES

1.

2.

3.

4.

5.

6.

7.

8.

YOUR
BUSINESS

About the author

Damión Hollomon is an author, music artist and app developer who was raised and currently resides in the Bay Area of Northern California. Graduating from Morris Brown College, he earned a Bachelor of Science degree in International Business. He is also co-founder and CEO of SmartPhoneRecords, a revolutionary mobile app created for artists which allows them to upload and sell their music straight from a smartphone.

Keep us updated!

We hope you enjoyed reading Shut Up and Startup. Let us know how it worked for you and keep us informed on your business progress at info@shutupandstartupbook.com

To join our mailing list and get updates on new releases, deals, bonus content and other business offering visit us online at www.ShutUpandStartupBook.com

You can also follow on twitter @shutupstartbook

To book Damión for public speaking engagements, book signings or workshops e-mail: booking@damionhollomon.com